Tom Bamberger

ABOUT THE AUTHOR

JOHN KOETHE is Distinguished Professor of Philosophy at the University of Wisconsin–Milwaukee, and the first Poet Laureate of Milwaukee. His collection *Falling Water* won the Kingsley Tufts Award. *North Point North: New and Selected Poems* was a finalist for the Los Angeles Times Book Prize. In 2005 he was a fellow of the American Academy in Berlin, and in 2008 he was the Elliston Poet in Residence at the University of Cincinnati. In 2010 he will be the Bain-Swiggett Professor of Poetry at Princeton University.

NINETY-FIFTH STREET

NINETY-FIFTH STREET

STREET

→ POEMS ←

JOHN KOETHE

HARPER ● PERENNIAL

NEW YORK ● LONDON ● TORONTO ● SYDNEY ● NEW DELHI ● AUCKLAND

HARPER ● PERENNIAL

NINETY-FIFTH STREET. Copyright © 2009 by John Koethe. All rights reserved. Printed in the United States of America. No part of this book may be used or reproduced in any manner whatsoever without written permission except in the case of brief quotations embodied in critical articles and reviews. For information address HarperCollins Publishers, 10 East 53rd Street, New York, NY 10022.

HarperCollins books may be purchased for educational, business, or sales promotional use. For information please write: Special Markets Department, HarperCollins Publishers, 10 East 53rd Street, New York, NY 10022.

FIRST EDITION

Designed by Ruth Lee-Mui

Library of Congress Cataloging-in-Publication Data
Koethe, John.
Ninety-fifth street : poems / John Koethe.— 1st Harper Perennial ed.
p. cm.
ISBN 978-0-06-176823-1
I. Title. II. Title: Ninety-fifth street.
PS3561.O35N56 2009
811'.54—dc22
2008055427

09 10 11 12 13   OV/RRD   10 9 8 7 6 5 4 3 2 1

To Douglas Crase

And in memory of Darragh Park

CONTENTS

ACKNOWLEDGMENTS

The poems in this book have appeared in the following journals or magazines:

American Scholar: "Belmont Park"
Berlin Journal: "Clouds"
Boston Review: "North Cambridge"
Cincinnati Review: "The Menomonee Valley"
Gulf Coast: "This Is Lagos"
Kenyon Review: "The Distinguished Thing," "These Magic
    Moments"
Literary Imagination: "The Recluse"
Margie: "Creation Myths"
Northwest Review: "The Lath House"
Poetry: "Chester," "Ninety-fifth Street," "Venetian Coda"
Poetry Northwest: "Karl-Marx-Allee," "On Happiness,"
    "Persistent Feelings"
Raritan: "European Love Story," "Potsdam," "The Yacht
    Clubs"
Smartish Pace: "Fear of the Future"
Southwest Review: "The Adagio"

Tight: " 'As I Woke Up One Morning' "
Yale Review: "Home"

"Chester" was recorded for the Poetry Foundation's film series
  Poetry Everywhere.
"Karl-Marx-Allee" and "North Cambridge" were reprinted on
  the Web site *Poetry Daily.*
"This Is Lagos" draws on an article by George Packer, "The
  Megacity," that appeared in *The New Yorker,* and a review
  by Charles Taylor of Jonathan Lear's *Radical Hope* that
  appeared in the *New York Review of Books.*
The poem "Ninety-fifth Street" contains numerous allusions
  to and quotations from other poems, not all of them
  explicit. I should mention that in particular the closing
  lines of the poem incorporate phrases from poems by
  Kenneth Koch ("To Marina"), Frank O'Hara ("Poem (Now
  the violets are all gone . . .)"), and John Ashbery ("The
  Skaters").

  I am grateful for a fellowship from the American Academy in Berlin, where the poems in section II were written; to the University of Cincinnati, where I was the Elliston Poet in Residence when this book was completed; to *Poetry Northwest* for awarding their Theodore Roethke Award to "On Happiness" and "Persistent Feelings"; and to David Schloss for help in arranging the book.

I

CHESTER

Wallace Stevens is beyond fathoming, he is so strange; it
is as if he had a morbid secret he would rather perish than
disclose . . .

—Marianne Moore to William Carlos Williams

Another day, which is usually how they come:
A cat at the foot of the bed, noncommittal
In its blankness of mind, with the morning light
Slowly filling the room, and fragmentary
Memories of last night's video and phone calls.
It is a feeling of sufficiency, once menaced
By the fear of some vague lack, of a simplicity
Of self, a self without a soul, the nagging fear
Of being someone to whom nothing ever happens.
Thus the fantasy of the narrative behind the story,
Of the half-concealed life that lies beneath
The ordinary one, made up of ordinary mornings

More alike in how they feel than what they say.
They seem like luxuries of consciousness,
Like second thoughts that complicate the time
One simply wastes. And why not? Mere being
Is supposed to be enough, without the intricate
Evasions of a mystery or offstage tragedy.
Evenings follow on the afternoons, lingering in
The living room and listening to the stereo
While Peggy Lee sings "Is That All There Is?"
Amid the morning papers and the usual
Ghosts keeping you company, but just for a while.
The true soul is the one that flickers in the eyes
Of an animal, like a cat that lifts its head and yawns
And looks at you, and then goes back to sleep.

HOME

It was a real place: There was a lawn to mow
And boxes in the garage. It was always summer
Or school, and even after oh so many years
It was always there, like the voice on the telephone
Each Sunday evening. I wondered how it was going to feel
When I was finally on my own—alone, with no family left
And no home to gravitate away from or think through.
I miss the trips I took each year to see my father.
I miss the desert and the ocean and the bungalows,
The drive up to L.A. to visit Rogers, yet all these feelings—
Are they actually feelings of loss, or just nostalgias for a notion?
I live in the same world, I inhabit the same life,
And yet it all seems insignificant and small. All that's left
Are the sensations of the empty afternoon, of feeling resigned
To the way things simply come and go, almost relieved
To find it almost feels like nothing. It feels like nothing at all.

THE LATH HOUSE

. . . breathing a small breath.

—Theodore Roethke

1853 (it sounds like a year) First Avenue,
The first house I remember that we lived in as a family.
Oh, there was the bungalow on Maxim Street we rented
While my father was in Korea, where I first discovered dreams,
And before that one in Hollywood I can barely remember,
A few blocks from Grauman's Chinese Theater.
This one had green awnings in the front, a living room
With Venetian blinds, a backyard with a garden and a pepper tree,
A small apartment over the garage, and behind all that
An unused lath house filled with dried-out dirt and vegetation,
Where the sunlight filtered weakly through the slats.
There was a shed with windows of translucent Plexiglass
Attached to it in back, with more decaying plants
Amid the spiders and the shadows. I hated going there:

It wasn't frightening so much as claustrophobic and unclear,
Like something difficult to see, then harder to recall.
What I remember most of all are houses, like the large
Victorian manse on Fir Street that I loved to paint
With watercolors, just across the street from where I stayed
When I had chicken pox, with my mother away at work
And my father away again in Japan, with an elderly retired couple—
What *was* their name?—who reminded me of Martha Hoople and
    the Major.

I love the way remembering lets the light in, as the sullen gray
Of consciousness dissolves into a yard, a pepper tree, a summer day,
And minor moments and details that had been buried in the past
Take on the clarity of dreams, with a transparency they never had
    in life.
—It isn't true. Some moments lie beyond the light, like the twins
My sister swears that she remembers when they came home from
    the hospital,
Who lived with us awhile before they died. They're just a blank to me:
It must have been on Maxim Street, and yet there's nothing there.
Sometimes an image of two figures in a crib seems just about to jell,
But it never sets, and then it melts away. I try to see my life
As a single narrative, with parts already there, and others to be
    filled in
By long chains of association, or the crumbling of a madeleine.
I can't believe that some of them are gone, as if they'd never
    happened—
Like another person's life, or one that flows in parallel with mine
Along its separate course, made up of the redacted parts

Like the dark matter making up the universe, or the averted face
That slowly turns to you at the climax of a nightmare, as a
    scream starts.

The neighborhood is gone. Long after we had moved away
There was a fire (I think), and then a freeway through downtown.
Somehow I've saved enough of it to re-create that world,
However incompletely: vacant lots where I caught butterflies
And shot birds with a BB gun whose cocking handle
Smashed my fingers once outside the watercolor house;
The walks home from St. Joseph's in my corduroys and cardigan;
The "Mad Dog! Mad Dog!" chasing me along a wall—
I don't need all of them to know those parts were real. The end
Of Catholic school, the start of physics, track, my father's nervous
    breakdown
All lay in the future. I've gone back to other places where I've lived,
But I can't go there now, which makes it seem the most mysterious
    of all.
The airplanes coming in for landings at the airport flew so low
That you could see the pilots from the roof, and lying there in
    the dark
I'd worry that a Russian bomber was descending to destroy us all.
When Nana died I remember listening to my parents murmuring softly
In the early morning darkness as my father packed for Texas
And I wondered if she'd burn in hell because she was a Baptist.
A morbid child? I hope not, though how would I know?
It was all about eternity—a modest one perhaps, but still eternity.
I wish the presence of the everyday could be enough,

The proximity of something small, and breathing a small breath.
It isn't though: it's something incomplete, like a mind half dead
   to itself
—"You don't *remember* them?"—lingering in the stippled
Shadows of the lath house, in the darkness of the shed behind it.

BELMONT PARK

I can only get there in a dream now,
In a poem. The streets and alleys to the south of it
Are still a bit seamy, and the Beachcomber
Is still a dive smelling of beer and urine,
But the real estate is simply worth too much
For any lingering seediness to last for long.
The asphalt boardwalk that used to run along the beach
Is smooth concrete now, and the tattoo parlors
And magazine shops with boxes full of dirty pictures
Are all gone too, along with the shooting galleries
Where you could win a watch guaranteed to fall apart in a week.
There was a public swimming pool called the Plunge
That smelled strongly of chlorine, in a pavilion with Moorish
Overtones, California-style. The dominating feature
Was a towering wooden roller coaster (it *felt* towering anyway)
That always looked rickety and on the verge of collapse.
We'd drive across some bridges and channels, past some phony
Polynesian hotels not far from where my aunt and uncle lived,

And on into Sunday afternoon: warm sand, cold waves
Burning your eyes and filling your mouth with sand, and big bulbs
    of kelp
Stranded on a waterline that constantly receded and flowed back.
I loved the California hamburgers (we never called them that)
    we'd order
As the night got louder and the lights got brighter. Then it was time
    to go home.

The poem knows where it's going—I could almost phone it in: a
    California
Past still lingering in a Raymond Chandler reverie, and then the air
    it wears today.
I have a photograph of myself in front of their house in La Jolla
My son took when we were home nine years ago, before my
    father died
And all those mental photographs I'd saved began to disappear.
I guess what's left is mine by definition, reaching all the way
To where the endlessness begins, the way the sand does to
    the sea.
I think of it as home, and yet there isn't much that I remember—
Maybe some palm trees, and the backstreets on the way to
    Crystal Pier,
Which has a Web site now, with FAQs and Cottage Photos—
Though it feels the same: confusing and banal and new
On the surface, concealing something old and waiting in the dark
When I go to sleep, or in my imagination as I wander across
    the years

And down a boulevard alive with bicycles and skateboards,
Lined with coffee and taco shops, that runs by the amusement
    park.

I like to think there's something vaster than myself
Hidden in the past, to be rekindled by a word—although I know
It's merely hidden in my brain, and by the time it filters through
    the cells
And nerves and finds the air, I've no idea where it came from.
I don't care for poetry readings—I never get the poems,
Though I'm curious about the poet—but at a Woodland Pattern
    reading
Sunday before last I heard a poem that pictured an abandoned
    amusement park
On a frozen coast in Sweden, near the Baltic Sea. I imagined ice
    and sand
Blowing through the skeleton of a Ferris wheel, and the broken
    boards
Of the refreshment stands that sold cool drinks in summer. I
    pictured Belmont Park
As it began to feel to me—a ruin waiting at the end of time,
Although I know time never really ends. I think of it as *my* time,
As I think of history as my life, because they feel the same.
The neighborhoods and parks that I grew up in alter and evolve
To suit the pleasures of the current age. The ones I keep in my heart
Decay, and come apart with age, and finally cease to be.
I'm happy in my life. A breeze floats off the lake
That stands in for an ocean, and there's a peculiar pleasure

Thinking about a Sunday on the beach, with my family all around
And the music of a calliope and the sound of a carousel
And the noise of popguns in the distance. They seem so close,
Like sounds floating across water—across a sea of love,
And then another sea—reaching endlessly away.

FEAR OF THE FUTURE

In the end one simply withdraws
From others and time, one's own time,
Becoming an imaginary Everyman
Inhabiting a few rooms, personifying
The urge to tend one's garden,
A character of no strong attachments
Who made nothing happen, and to whom
Nothing ever actually happened—a fictitious
Man whose life was over from the start,
Like a diary or a daybook whose poems
And stories told the same story over
And over again, or no story. The pictures
And paintings hang crooked on the walls,
The limbs beneath the sheets are frail and cold
And morning is an exercise in memory
Of a long failure, and of the years
Mirrored in the face of the immaculate
Child who can't believe he's old.

THE RECLUSE

Nothing gets finished, and so much
Is never even begun, dogging your life forever.
No one wants to be like someone else,
For each one thinks he's special, and indeed he is.
Friend, I speak to you from Vernon Manor
In Cincinnati, where the Beatles stayed
When they played America over forty years ago.
My life is your life. What I want to say to you
Is what you'd say to me if I were you and you were me,
Which I know is impossible, and makes no sense.
It's been raining off and on all day. I've stayed in my room
Reading a book about the bamboo fly rod, musing on *The Prelude*
And the even longer poem of which it was to be a kind of coda—
"O let it be the tail-piece of *The Recluse*," Coleridge wrote,
"For of nothing but *The Recluse* can I hear patiently." Wordsworth
Never wrote it. His idea of God became more orthodox
As he aged into a public figure, the identity of God and Nature
And the sense of the sublime that it occasioned
Fading away, becoming just another part of His design,
The freshness of the language lost, becoming—

What? Not more self-absorbed (that was hardly possible),
But self-absorbed in an increasingly distant way.
We know what happened to *The Prelude.*

I remember reading the poem about the daffodils
In high school, just around the time I started floating
· Gently down those streams of consciousness
Where modernism chronicled the dissolving soul—
The old inside the new, uneasily together in a spot of time,
A trick of consciousness the mind plays on itself.
I remember spending a whole summer working on a poem
That ended with a prospect of some floating mountains
Defining the world, contained (to steal a phrase)
In an "imagination of the whole" that seemed to coalesce
"Above this frame of things," before it disappeared
Into a blizzard of confused perceptions. It's all so
Strange now: visions and deflating theories come and go,
And yet whatever they concern remains unchanged. The rain
Descends on Vernon Manor, where I'm waiting for a phone call,
Wondering what had made it once seem so important. Was it
Simply a desire to be different—to not be someone else, to not be
Something else? "You are an *I*," I heard a voice exclaiming, "you are an
Elizabeth, you are one of *them. Why* should you be one, too?"
To be an object in a world of things: it's what the recluse fears,
And what his argument portends. The face in the mirror
Might be anyone's or no one's, slowly becoming dead to itself,
Like a word's becoming meaningless through repetition.
I want to hear the Beatles. I could look up what they played
When they played here (you can find nearly anything on the Web),

But there's no CD player in my room. I have my bamboo
Rod to fool around with, but I've done that a few times already,
And might as well save it for the future, or at least next week.
Meanwhile I think I might have talked myself into a poem,
Waiting out the weeks in a hotel room in a small city
Far from home, as the rain is ending and it's time for bed.

ON HAPPINESS

It's a simple question, and I even know what it is
Until you ask me, as Augustine said of time.
It's either too commonplace or too rare, an esoteric condition
You could spend your life attaining, or a waste of time.

Plato thought of it as a kind of balance in the soul
Between its three parts (though he called it something else),
And Freud thought along the same lines, in his role
As the first happiness therapist, only called it unhappiness

Of the ordinary kind. Wittgenstein said the happy
And unhappy man inhabit two completely different worlds,
While Mill equated it with pleasures of all kinds,
From high to low, from the pleasure mirrored in a young girl's

Smile to the consolations of the scholar in his cave.
I'd go on, but you can see the problem: a question posed
A long time ago, to which different people gave
Such different answers, answers concerning different things.

"What *is* X anyway?" I know the sensible course
Would be to drop those kinds of questions, and just stumble along
Whatever road you'd taken, taking the moments as they come.
Yet some of them have been a part of me for so long—

That race, the picnic at the Institute, the night of the science fair.
Were all those moments the fulfillment of some plan
Or deep attachment, however trivial, or of some abiding care?
Is that what it is—the feeling of a life brought to fruition

On its own terms, whatever terms it chose?
It sounds free, and yet it's rife with opportunities for self-delusion
And bad faith, like the pool of water out of sunlight in the rose-garden,
An epiphany that seems, in retrospect, like a studied illusion.

Was Ariel happy that he'd written all those poems?
He said so, yet beneath them you can almost sense the fear
Of having lived a skeleton's life, in a world of bones.
Perhaps it's best to stay at home and read,

Instead of risking everything for what in the end
Might be of no more significance than a fascinating hobby,
Like collecting bottle caps, or building ships in bottles.
There are smaller choices to be made: hanging about the lobby

Of a W Hotel vs. watching the Great Downer Avenue Bike Race
From Dave's front porch. Why do we feel the need to create ourselves
Through what we choose, instead of simply sinking without a trace
Into the slow stream of time? The evening light is lovely

On the living room wall, with a gentle touch of green
Reflected from the trees outside. I realize it feels like a letdown
To be told that this is all it comes to—a pleasant apartment
On a shady street a few miles north of downtown,

And yet it isn't all that bad: it offers concrete satisfactions
In lieu of whatever happiness might be; and though I worry that it's
Something I've backed into, at least it's free from the distractions
Of the future, and seems fine for now. As for a deeper kind

Of happiness, if there is such a thing, I'll take a rain check.
We could go shopping for those dishes, try out the new
Pancake House around the corner, or grill something on the deck
And watch a movie. I guess that's what we should do.

PERSISTENT FEELINGS

Sometimes I'm driving, and the highway
Fades into the sky, into the music I've got on
—Mark Knopfler or the *Quine Tapes*—
And the earth becomes a planet, and a funny spell
Falls over me, a bittersweet, unfocused thrill.
And sometimes here at home I feel it too,
Although less vividly: a calm elation tinctured with
A sense of loss—not because someone left
Or died, or someone wasn't loved,
Hard as those things are, but simply at having lived
For now, and only for now. The light is golden
And the lawns are green. The street hides its mysteries
From time's deflating gaze: clear eyed and free,
Emotionless, yet filled with feelings of a deeper kind,
Ones that flow without saying. The afternoon
Is full of memories and silent passions,
Though there's nothing in particular to see:
No children in the leaves, no faces hidden in the trees
Or signs to show the presence or the absence of the gods.
Feelings should be personal, though they needn't be:

Besides the mild disappointments and the ordinary pleasures
Each day brings, the hurt time heals, there's the wonder
That this life exists at all, that something as familiar as the sky
Could persist in my absence, that the present is the limit of the life
In which I find myself and feel, deep inside a space
Filled with my own breath, the exhilaration and unspoken
Sadness of a world—my world, the only world—
Held together by memory, that ends at death.

THE MENOMONEE VALLEY

It was always the first thing Geoff wanted to see
Whenever he'd drive over from Madison to visit me.
He saw it as the quintessential landscape
Of the Essential City, by contrast with that ersatz one

Some eighty miles away, the juvenile capital
Of record stores and gyro joints and bubble gum.
It splits Milwaukee into South and North, the factories,
The bungalows and taverns of the men who used to work in them

Vs. what remains of downtown, the Pfister Hotel, the lakefront
And the mansions of the millionaires who used to own them.
In early spring it's still a nearly frozen wasteland
Of railroad tracks and smokestacks and a narrow, dull canal

Flowing past slag heaps flecked with scraps of snow and seagulls.
Down the road from Badger Bumper, the Miller Compressing
    Company
Flattens what's left over of the cars, then lifts them up and

Dumps them on a monumental mountain of aluminum and steel,
To be pulverized at last into a kind of coarse, toxic metal meal.
Yet even wastelands change. The noxious smells
That used to permeate the air are gone. The Milwaukee Stockyards
Where we'd stop for lunch (there was a funny restaurant there)

Left town two years ago. The Peck Meat Packing plant
Is rationality itself, with trucks with modern logos and an antiseptic
    air.
The Tannery, an "Urban Business and Living Center"
Lodged inside the shells of what were once some of the foulest

Factories in the country, is the first stage of a plan
To redefine this "huge forlorn Brownfield" into a different kind of
    space,
A place of "offices, light manufacturing, a riverfront bike trail"
Meant to ease the lingering traces of a vanishing industrial sublime.

→ ←

Geoff moved to California, where he shot himself in 1987.
Growing up in San Diego, I would linger at the list of fifty largest
    cities
In the *World Book*, San Diego down there near the bottom
And Milwaukee floating somewhere towards the top. The tallest
    building

Was the El Cortez Hotel, eight stories high. Lane Field,
Where the Padres played, stood at the foot of Broadway, near the
    harbor

And the tattoo parlors and the shops purveying cheap civilian clothes.
I remember listening to the Yankees and the Braves in 1958

On my new transistor radio, and dreaming of the day I'd move away—
Which I did when I was seventeen, just before the country
Started changing, before everything I used to take for granted
Started turning into photographs, and to disappear.

You hardly noticed it at first, the demographics shifting
Imperceptibly, the cities on the list displaced by bland
    southwestern
Sunlight, like the sunlight in Miami at Geoff's funeral.
When I'd go back to visit there were ever taller towers,

Glassed-in skyscrapers that seemed to all be banks.
A freeway turned Pacific Highway into just another throughway
Running past the empty Convair factory, which had closed.
I used to love the seedy section south of Broadway,

With the joke shop next door to the Hollywood Burlesque,
The pawnshops where I'd look at microscopes, and San Diego
    Hardware,
Where I'd buy materials for the science fair. Like the stockyards,
All that's history now: I heard on NPR last week

The hardware store was moving to the suburbs, driven away
By high rents and a parking shortage in the Gaslamp District, a
    pathetic

Exercise in urban fantasy designed to recreate a picturesque
Historic neighborhood you think is real, but never actually existed.

➔ ←

My father's story started in a little town in Texas, Henrietta—
Growing up, then going away to school in Oklahoma,
Juilliard in New York, playing with some orchestras in Europe,
Entering the Navy at the start of WWII, and finally dying of a
    stroke

About five years ago in San Diego—taken at the end
From Naval Hospital to a quiet hospice overlooking Mission Valley.
It's so much vaster than Menomonee, and yet the moral and the
    landscape
Seem essentially the same: the minor narratives of individual lives

Played out against a background of relentless change. On my last
    visit,
Driving down the hill on Texas Street, it seemed to open out
Into a vision of the city of the future: Qualcomm Stadium on the
    right
And Fashion Valley on the left, and spilling over from its floor

And flowing up the farther side, generic condominiums as far as I
    could see,
Like the ones along the river in Milwaukee. It's as though the dream
Were just to leave those individual lives behind, in all their
    particularity
And local aspirations, their constraints and disappointments,

•   •   •

For a thin reality that offers fantasies and limitless degrees of
   freedom—
And for *what*? Sometimes I wonder if it's just finance and entropy,
Although I know that can't be true. Traffic flows in all directions
Through the valleys and across the country, on a grid of possibilities

To be realized in turn, and then abandoned. People move away
   from home
And die, and the places where they'd lived and whiled away the time
Are temporary, like the units of a mathematical sublime
Reducing what had been a country of localities and neighborhoods

To a bare concept, an abstraction that extends "from sea to shining sea,"
The silence in its fields of derelict machinery and rusting metal
Broken by the din of new construction, as an all-consuming history
Proceeds apace beneath an n-dimensional, indifferent sky.

CLOUDS

I love the insulation of strange cities:
Living in your head, the routines of home
Becoming more and more remote,
Alone and floating through the streets
As through the sky, anonymous and languageless
Here at the epicenter of three wars. Yesterday
I took the S-Bahn into town again
To see the Kiefer in the Neue Nationalgalerie,
A burned-out field with smoke still rising from the furrows
In a landscape scarred with traces of humanity
At its most brutal, and yet for all that, traces of humanity.
What makes the world so frightening? In the end
What terrifies me isn't its brutality, its violent hostility,
But its indifference, like a towering sky of clouds
Filled with the wonder of the absolutely meaningless.
I went back to the Alte Nationalgalerie
For one last look at its enchanting show of clouds—
Constable's and Turner's, Ruskin's clouds and Goethe's
Clouds so faint they're barely clouds at all, just lines.
There was a small glass case that held a panel

Painted by the author of a book I'd read when I was twenty-five—
Adalbert Stifter, *Limestone*—but hadn't thought about in years.
Yet there were Stifter's clouds, a pale yellow sky
Behind some shapes already indistinct (and this was *yesterday*),
As even the most vivid words and hours turn faint,
Turn into memories, and disappear. Is that so frightening?
Evanescence is a way of seeming free, free to disappear
Into the background of the city, of the sky,
Into a vast surround indifferent to these secret lives
That come and go without a second thought
Beyond whatever lingers in some incidental lines,
Hanging for a while in the air like clouds
Almost too faint to see, like Goethe's clouds.

EUROPEAN LOVE STORY

Words *can* describe it, though not very well.
Instead, it simply looks or smells a certain way,
If a picture could be said to smell. You
Settle into your seat as the lights go down
And you're in a small town in Poland or Germany.
A guy walks down a street, or falls in love with a girl.
A held breath is everywhere, death is in the air,
And love is too, though it's finally death that predominates.
Off to one side there are train tracks, unused now,
Though everyone knows where they used to go.
A light rain falls, but it never dissolves the smell
Of skin and disinfectant, of something poised to begin
In the outbuildings of corrugated metal and crumbling brick.
They meet on a train, then again at someone's house.
The narrative unfolds with the force of fate,
While its meaning remains entirely on the surface,
Disarmingly literal, maddeningly incomplete, concluding
With a letter in a case in a museum, and a picture

Of a girl with blond hair and the sweetest smile—evil enough,
And still more evil as the years go by, becoming at last
A true story, though everyone knows where it goes:
Falling in love with a girl. A guy walking down a street.

THE YACHT CLUBS

. . . and the holocaust was complete.

—*The Great Gatsby*

Like a question in a dream
Whose answer lies across the water
In a green light of hope, in a slow scream
Beginning with a single breath
Exhaled in a dining room beneath a tapestry . . .
What happens is the stuff of history.
What lingers is the new reality
Of photographs and printed words, coalescing
Into colors in the dark behind closed eyes:
The greens of hope, the yellows and pinks of death.

The passage from the hatred in the heart
To the absurd, from passion to the nearly empty day,
Like the reductio ad absurdum of some plan—

What starts in fantasy or fear becomes
A sky of softly colored clouds
Whose simple beauty mirrors nothing,
Whose indifference is a way of understanding
The banality not of evil, but of romance
In the old sense, of complexity and art, as the past
Unfolds into an ordinary future, year by year . . .

The surface of the water is alive with waves.
The bus leaves from the Bahnhof, driving west
Across a bridge and towards a nursery
Selling hothouse flowers and shrubs. Here and there
It stops for passengers, pausing at a corner
Where amid the lowering anxiety of the afternoon,
The sense of something breathing in the air
Above the marker for the Haus der Wannsee-Conferenz,
It suddenly turns right and begins a slow descent
Along the road that leads to the yacht clubs.

CREATION MYTHS

Some have the grandeur of architecture,
The grandeur of the concert hall: the sentimental
Grandeur of an idea lying just beyond recall
In someone's imagination, compelled by an even
Greater music at its most monumental,
That begins with the explosion of a drum
In chaos and the dark, the twin wellsprings of a world
That slowly comes to lie before them—a natural
One, apparently designed for them alone,
That somehow lifts them in the end, a woman and a man,
To Paradise and the certainty of God.

It's lovely to believe—lovely, anyway, to hear.
The chaos is still there, but rather than a distant state
From which the patterns of this life emerged,
It feels like part of it, like sex or sleep,
The complex workings of a dream made visible.
This afternoon I took the S-Bahn into town,
Getting off at a half-completed shell
In the middle of what felt like nowhere,

One stop before the Friederichstrasse station.
I picked my way along a maze of barriers and fences,
Down an open street and past a makeshift balcony
Overlooking a pit, the site of the creation
Of the Hauptbahnhof to come. It was *echt* Berlin:
A panorama filled with transcendental buildings to the south,
And in the foreground towering red and yellow cranes
Branded with the initials *DB*, a cacophony
Assembled to articulate some inarticulate design,
But closer to the truth: a half-baked world,
The perfect setting for a half-baked life.
I used to think one finished what the past began,
Instead of moving things around inside a no-man's-land,
A landscape always on the verge, always unrealized . . .

Purpose and design; a sort of purpose, with a form
Still waiting to emerge; and finally, lack of any
Strategy or plan, as entropy increases—
On my way back from a puzzling museum
I found myself rehearsing various ideas of order
And disorder, ideas of intent, deliberation, and control.
Three hours earlier, strolling through its galleries
Full of different kinds of cocks, encaustic cunts and oddly moving
Piles of junk from the Berlin equivalent of OfficeMax
Or Home Depot, all strewn about the floor
Of what until the war had been a neo-Renaissance
Train station, I'd suddenly felt the wonder of uncertainty
At how these things so stubbornly neglected to emerge
From the rubble of Creation's threshing floor,

But simply lay there—*all this stuff*—deliberately chosen,
I suppose, yet out of context signifying nothing but themselves.
I'd felt absurdly happy. Maybe it was the notion
That the realm of the imaginary coincided with the present,
With an ordinary day spent wandering here and there,
And later on that evening, *The Creation* at the Philharmonie.
At any rate, I'd seen enough. There was no place else
I especially wanted to go—no more exhibitions
Or architecture—and nothing I particularly wanted to do
—Window-shopping in the stores along the Ku'damm—
And so I wandered through its massive doors
Into the afternoon and the museum of the future.

KARL-MARX-ALLEE

When I try to picture Europe in the wake
Of WWII, I think of Slothrop disappearing in the Zone,
Or a dull sky and a wide street stretching away
Like the corridor of trees at the end of *The Third Man*.
The truth is less dramatic, for instead of programs
And the clash of vast ideas, there's the tedium
And minor infelicities of daily life, its infinite detail
Before it simplifies and settles into history.
Karl-Marx-Allee runs east from Alexanderplatz
Towards the towers at the Frankfurter Tor, with all the drama
And authority that history used to seem to have.
It has the feel of a heroic boulevard, with walks on either side
Protected by a canopy of trees and lined with socialist
Apartment blocks you're not supposed to like, although I do.
What was it *like* before the Wall, before the Wall came down—
Not in the abstract or the large, but day by day?
I think it was essentially the same—getting up each day
To the next reality, a world of shrinking aspirations
Limited, more or less, to what you already had.
It all sounds small and real, yet is that actually so bad?

Was it worse than all those grotesque dreams
That seemed to beckon from the capitals beyond the Wall?
Of course one wanted to be free, but free from *what*?
From harm, which is the freedom children have?
From scrutiny, which is the empty freedom of the Zone?
The sense is just of moving on, refusing to look back
Until one day you find yourself alone and in a different century,
Obsessed by sentimental images of home, all sad.

My impressions of Berlin come mostly from a book
I read some forty years ago, *The Spy Who Came In from the Cold,*
That classic exposé of Cold War chess. The strategy of its game
Is hard to reconstruct, but what's stuck with me instead
Is a handful of snapshots: a labyrinth of empty streets at night;
Two figures in a spotlight crouched before the Wall
And then some shots; a family laughing in a minuscule car
The moment when it's crushed between two huge, converging trucks.
It's hard to see beyond them, looking backwards
Through a programmatic lens at those monotonous facades,
And in the West the gilded concert halls and subsidized boutiques.
My first week in Berlin I watched the movie of that book
In my apartment—just some images at first, without the sound
To give them context, or explain what I was looking at might mean.
I take the train to town each day and walk around. Some days
I stumble through a tour from an architectural guidebook
I can barely read beyond the names of buildings and their dates.
Last week I wandered through a tour in the East, with light snow
Falling as I made my way past the ubiquitous apartments and a *Kino.*
Suddenly, in a far corner of Strausberger Platz, I came upon

A bust of Marx, standing in a little grove of evergreens
And looking out unseeing on the busy boulevard that bears his name.
Across the street a man stood on a balcony with plants,
Consumed by thought or daydreaming—it was impossible to tell.
He retreated to the privacy of his bedroom or his kitchen,
As I'd have done myself, back at what is home for now in Wannsee.
People memorize themselves, and try to live that way
Forever, seeking refuge from the great, surrounding storms
In lives inscrutable and self-contained as jars.
I see the future every day. It works all right I guess,
Yet offers no suggestion of the overall design
To which our lives—*our* lives—belong, as each proceeds apace
Here in the realm of ends, a street comprising isolated
Songs whose melodies unfold within the confines of a room,
And families driving somewhere in their cars.

POTSDAM

One day your poem comes to the little city
Where they made those movies, and then later
Got together and divided up the world.
You stroll into the weather and across a bridge
Into some version of the present, turning
At a corner to a cobbled street shut off from traffic
And alive with tourists, with an oversized
Department store, and at the other end a church.
It's like a story on the verge of making sense,
Before it suddenly pulls back to let the real story
Roll on someplace else; or like an afternoon
Spent wandering through the theme park
Looming at the end of history, a sullen place
Without ideas, but only things with various names
And nothing left to do but write them down
And hope that something different might
    emerge—
Some mix of the familiar and the strange,

Together as one—as the poem's paternal voice
Delivers its predictable reproach: stick to what is real,
My son, instead of all those diffident abstractions.
But was there ever a reality like that? Weren't
Blut, *Boden*, and *Juden* all abstractions too?

THE ADAGIO

Berlin has a familiar air. It isn't very old
As European cities go, and its amorphous sprawl
Reminds me just a little of Los Angeles—
A place without a single center, offering instead
A set of variations on a theme. With cranes
At its construction sites, graffiti blooming everywhere,
It seems to mask some underlying randomness
Or dream, one whose true significance remains unclear.
Where does the present start, if it isn't in the past?
How should someone set about to live
Within the shadows of another era's history?
These are questions left unasked, or hanging in the air
Above the Reichstag with its glass-and-metal dome
Sitting on the banks of the Spree. I walk its streets alone,
A mind that drifts across the surface of the day
As on a death march starting on the outskirts of the city,
Registering along the way the synagogues and camps,
The churches and the cemeteries, blending them together
Into one continuous breath, broken up by random
Moments of a private beauty, like the prayers of a devout,

Yet always shadowed by the consciousness of death,
Of beauty's darker underside, as in the filmed reconstruction
Of the conference at Wannsee when, as they're about to leave,
Heydrich puts a piece of Schubert's on the gramophone
And remarks to Eichmann, "The adagio will tear your heart out."

The city feels like that. You start to see connections
Everywhere, as though the fantasy that ended in a bunker
Sixty years ago had happened yesterday—a story
Buried in the morning papers, waiting at the grocery store
As people go about the business of the day. And art is everywhere
As well, and needs its stories too, and if today's seem too banal
Or dull it tries to find them in the air, in fragments
Of that null refrain whose truth lies largely in the telling.
Last week a violinist from the Philharmoniker had dinner here.
She'd settled in Berlin two months ago, and found it . . . well,
"Peculiar," in a word. With culture in the broadest sense
So dominant, and next to nothing to compare it to, it dwells,
She thought, reflexively upon its past, engendering an atmosphere
Of history and the dark whose self-sustaining animus is art.
I think she's mostly right. Sometimes I find myself surprised,
Turning from a book, or looking up to see the sky
Above the tombstones and the family plots at Weissensee,
Or walking down the alleyway that runs along the outer wall
At Sachsenhausen, to realize how fragile all this really is,
How much it draws on memory and the force of the imagination
Just to remain alive. For unless they answered to a need,
The slaughters of the past, along with what was tenderest and true,
Would disappear; unless a shared lament created a reality

Reflecting its own power, making a mythology
Of necessity . . . which may be what the violinist meant.

Spring has come to Wannsee. The ice has melted,
And the ferryboats are floating back and forth again.
It's colder in Milwaukee, and the sky isn't as blue,
But otherwise I think it's basically the same. We try
To tell ourselves that life is local, history is local,
But it isn't true: beneath the details a relentless urge to power
Waits unsleeping for a pretext—like the Reichstag fire,
The falling towers—to let its mindless march resume.
Last night before the reading I was standing on the balcony
Where Max Liebermann, who had the luck to die before the worst,
Watched them marching through the Brandenburger Tor in 1933.
He knew that it was over, that his world was over,
Though nothing *actual* had happened. That lay in the future,
Where the Conference House stood next door to his own.
It was all potential, like a composition waiting to be played.
The music flows so slowly, so inexorably
You hardly notice it at all. Truth is the first to go
—Minor truths at first, then ever greater ones—
Then memory and the personal past, and then the past.
It offers you a way of being free, but then the emptiness sets in—
The freedom of a life without a context, life inside a vacuum
In which none of it had happened, giving up at last
A notice in the newspaper, an announcement on the radio
That someone strains to hear behind the static,
Listening in the distance to the strains of the adagio.

VENETIAN CODA

Sometimes I dream what's called the *male dream*:
I'm going somewhere not too far away, I'm almost there,
When there's a slight delay—a minor detour of no consequence,
But then another, and another, as I get farther and farther
Away from my initial destination, which becomes inaccessible.
Before I left Berlin I went to Venice, a city that reminds me of
    that dream.
However close you are to where you want to go, the compound
Turnings of its narrow passageways and alleys carry you
    relentlessly away,
Until you dead-end at a small canal that's nowhere on your map.
The late, wrecked century that started in Berlin, where all roads lead—
I thought I'd find, if not the truth exactly, then at least an inkling
Of some fantasy that lay beneath the placid surface of the day,
The remnants of some dream so many people had to die for. Instead
I watched the boats go by, and clouds traverse the sky
Above an unreal city floating on the water. We're sure at first
That something lies beyond the facts and books, but then we realize
    it isn't there.

Whatever lay behind that slaughter wasn't in the world,
Existing merely in the heart, in memory, in someone's imagination,
Places harboring nothing real. To try to see it is to watch it disappear,
Stranding you a life away from where the unimaginable began,
Staring blankly at your own face floating in the water.

"AS I WOKE UP ONE MORNING"

As I woke up one morning
In my solitary bed,
The colors of a delicious dream
Flickered a while in my head

Before fading into day
And the early-morning news
Of someone waiting for a promise
Of the life that time renews,

Even as it takes away.
The day stretched out before me
Like a duty waiting to be kept,
Like something boundless and free

And yet to be completed
By what sleep left in its wake—
To come back as something beautiful,
To be loved for its own sake

And for the love it might bring.
I heard the hint of a song
As I lingered before the mirror,
Sure that before very long

It would all feel new again,
If only for a few hours,
By dint of an inconsolable
Imagination's powers

Of transcending time and space
Before falling back to earth.
Like a king who travels from afar
To be present at a birth

That in its "hard and bitter
Agony" seems more like death,
I was the sovereign of my kingdom
Of one room, where every breath

Brought me nearer to the tomb.
The paths of least resistance
Lead to dead ends. I thought I saw it
Beckoning in the distance

Like a friend just out of reach.
Why are poems and life so hard?
Is there a place where the forgotten
Things I'd labored to discard

Might still be waiting for me?
You who listens and pretends
To care about these abject musings
On which my whole life depends,

Do they mean that much to you?
Wouldn't you prefer instead
Brief entertainments to pass the time
Until the time comes for bed?

In the dream I'd had that night
—And oh! to have it again—
Something seemed to answer from the air
Like a life poised to begin,

As the words found their places
On a page, and in the gloom
The gold gathered the light against it,
And you were there in my room.

THE DISTINGUISHED THING

Here it is at last, the distinguished thing.

—Henry James

It needn't start with reading
—Though it does—but with an opening
So sweet and self-sustaining that it lasts forever,
A chapter out of all proportion to its years.
Then come those long, perplexing middle parts
I still can't figure out, years that in retrospect
Went by so quickly that I find myself astonished
To see where I am now, on a February day
In my sixty-second year, watching some specks of light
Float before my eyes like small bright snowflakes,
And then disappear. The floating life is next,
An infinite vacation where the days repeat themselves
As in the movie *Groundhog Day*, and time has lost its meaning.

What did they mean, the ones who cautioned us to wait

For all the wishes from the opening to be granted at the end?

Bent over a computer in a study filled with catalogs and magazines,

My life is fine, though not the life I'd wanted or imagined,

For instead of amplitude and progress there's the slow refinement

Of a figure that was there from the beginning, like a pattern in a carpet.

The background is the monochrome from which it sprang,

The null "one color" into which it quietly disappears

On a dull winter day or a warm November afternoon

In a room in sight of the ocean. A life creates a world

That coincides with it, a world in which its narrative unfolds

In all the rich detail that makes it seem so real. It flows from day
      to day,

Sometimes distracted by the scenery, haunted by the thought

Of something childlike and silent waiting at the end.

The bubble breaks, the figure on the screen dissolves

And leaves me sitting in a comfortable apartment

On a gray midwinter morning more than forty years from home.

I'd read for hours in the brown recliner chair

That sat in my bedroom next to the long row of windows

Giving on the street and canyon and some rudimentary mountains

Hiding an imaginary country that I made believe was home.

I fell for everything those stories said, the stories

Gathered in a Bennett Cerf anthology of "modern fiction"

Hidden in a closet in the hallway with a cookbook

And the *World Book* and *Vogue's Book of Etiquette.*

The leopard's carcass frozen in the snow; the sense of how things are

And how they ought to be, of what's expected or appropriate:
I wonder what I thought those stories *were*—a kind of esoteric
    knowledge
That would buoy me to the end? It's not that things go wrong
As you grow up, but that they get more complicated, as the
    certainties
Of seventeen dissolve into the seasons of maturity and doubt—
At least if by "maturity" you mean a sense of resignation,
An indifference to the way your prayers are always answered
When you least expect it, and you've ceased to care.
I felt like I was going home to college when I left,
Caught up in all those fictions of myself time decomposed.
Why do I always think of home as someplace else? Why do I feel,
Each time I go back to New York, a place I've never lived,
That I've returned? All tangled up together at the time,
They seem in retrospect like stages: marriage, Cambridge, moving
    here
And fatherhood, the shifting cast of friends, the stuff that poems
    are made on
Like the end of marriage and the growing dread of winding up alone,
As one by one your family dies and your career winds down.
It all seems literal and small: the marriage and the moving; the career,
The pension, the prescriptions; the stock banalities of age.
What is that simple truth I want to bring to mind, the truth that
    lies behind
The willful effort to invest these hours with the distant grandeur
Of a different age, and memories that are more about remembering
Than the world they try to re-create? That world is gone,
Supplanted by an unremarkable room where a person sits alone

And tells the story of his life to anyone who's interested, i.e., to no
    one,
For the others all have stories of their own. That leaves the waiting,
Waiting out the season while the afternoons begin to lengthen
One more time into those beautiful spring evenings, though for
    what?

There was a sudden lightness as the airplane landed. Ascending, it seemed that I could look down on my life as though for the first time, and see that all the possibilities I thought had been closed had been renewed. The past was as it was, but the future was indefinite, waiting to be filled with moments distilled from all the moments when I'd been most happy. I could see us sitting in LaGuardia in 1975, giddy from the weekend out at Bob's with Doug and Frank, and the evening afterwards at Darragh's, realizing simultaneously that the time was right for us to have a child. I could see myself waiting in that same space twelve years later, on a bright November morning after a dinner with Willy in the upstairs dining room at Frank's on Fourteenth Street, dumbstruck by the thought that turned into the last line of the poem I started in to write, "Why do I feel so happy?" And just twelve years ago, walking along Canal Street on a blue and blinding February morning, bleary from a wedding that had lasted until two, I felt absurdly happy to be back once more at what still felt like home, walking to my ritual Sunday lunch in Chinatown, then down to a deserted Wall Street, a part of the city I'd somehow never visited before. These moments happened long ago and not so long ago, yet as I gazed at them I realized the happiness that they'd afforded me was still available, still waiting to be experienced again. It was the opposite of the coda of *Swann's Way*, when the narrator, brooding on his own mortality, goes out one morning to a park that had remained for him the locus of an ideal world, dismayed to find that the emotions he'd experienced there had vanished, and existed only in his memory, like the carriages and fashions of another age. Instead of wishes, dreams, and disappointments, I felt the calm elation of surrendering to the moments, whatever they might hold, that were yet to come, and of not asking for more. Wittgenstein, in the "Lecture on Ethics," spoke of an experience of feeling "absolutely safe," of feeling that nothing could ever injure you, whatever happened, a thought he said was nonsense, though the experience and the feeling are completely real—real as this feeling of life aloft, of drifting day to day across the seasons towards a denouement to be arranged by chance, buoyed by an understanding of the possibilities to come, responding gaily, one fine morning, to obedient hands . . .

—Of course not. It takes awhile, or maybe years and years,
But the inevitable eventually arrives, perhaps on a Friday,
Despite some weekend plans, on the way to measure for curtains
Or buy furniture for a new apartment. Time slows down
And words become difficult, as you look around perplexed at where
    you are:
In a too warm room, under sheets that grab, in a gown worn thin
    and soft from laundering.
Figures come and go, bringing—what? At times it's dark, at other
    times it's light;
Sometimes the dark is broken by a nightlight and the hissing of an
    autoclave
Outside the room, or you're abandoned in a hallway, or a room
    overlooking a valley

And an ocean you can't see, unconscious of the photographs that
  someone must have left.
Why am I so maddened by all this? In the end a life is ordinary, in
  its intimate details
And in its underlying themes, including death. I had a vision once,
Which wasn't even mine, of a long breath bounded at its ends by silence,
Like a sentence following the story of a life until its energy was spent
And its parentheses closed. It's like the childish thought one tries to
  overcome,
But never does: that the ending must be true because it seems
  mysterious,
As indeed it is, which makes it such a final disappointment—
Like that thought that lingers for a while and disappears, or the vision
That comes to nothing in the end—the nothing that underlies
  experience
And until then had been merely an idea, of a distinguished thing.

THESE MAGIC MOMENTS

We were sitting on the terrace of a small hotel
On a side street in a town we'd never visited before.
I wrote this down:

> They drive around the square
> In cars they purchase out of petty cash
> And eat french-fried potatoes
> Wrapped up in little hats

Later we were sitting at a table on a glassed-in boat
As it floated down the Rhine. We ate dinner
And watched the steep vineyards glide by on the right,
And then we were in the Alps, surrounded by picturesque chalets
With window boxes filled with geraniums.

—This was a long time ago, in the Europe
In the mind, the Europe experienced for the first time,
Where you could ride from A to B without a second thought,
For nearly nothing. There are cheap flights now,

•   •   •

But it's not the same. I'm not the same,
Yet this is all I have to show for what I was—
I'm riding on a train, leafing through a guidebook
And looking out the window at some moments of my life
Rolling by to the melody of an old Drifters song,
And they seem like such a *waste* now,
A waste of time. All that's magic about them
Is that they were mine, and they're gone.

NORTH CAMBRIDGE

If it was good enough for Eliot to write about,
I guess it's good enough for me, although I only
Lived there for a year, on Dudley Street
At first, across from the trackless trolley yard.
It didn't suit my fantasies at all—the drab apartment
And my two unlikely roommates: Dan,
A counter-counterculture lawyer
Sprung from Harvard and South Boston,
Whom I'd meet most Fridays for a pub crawl
Culminating in dinner, when he'd rise to the occasion
To celebrate "the poor bastard on the bar stool";
And Eric, of indeterminate occupation
And a closet full of magazines of naked boys.
There was a bar on the corner (there was a bar on *every* corner)
Filled each morning with plenty of poor bastards on bar stools
(Night shift from the trolley?) drinking shots and ten-cent beers at 7 a.m.
I had a visit from a friend from college, Ed Kissam,
In town to give a reading for the *Advocate.* Ed's entourage

Consisted of a biker in full leather and a woman with a black beret
Who'd just been raped by rival bikers, which she took in stride.
The president of the *Advocate* wasn't sure just what to make of them,
But endured the evening anyway, and then we all retired—
Ed, the biker, Ms. Beret—to Dudley Street, and called up David Schatz,
My new best-friend-to-be, discovered to live a block away,
Who showed up wearing a purple satin Nehru shirt
À la John Lennon. You can imagine what Dan made of *that*—
Not to mention his house filled with these sixties clowns,
The air of drunken levity, the dope. Things deteriorated after that,
And I departed Dudley Street and moved to David's place
Around the corner on Mass Ave. Fall to winter
And a deepening war: Eugene McCarthy represented hope,
And Johnson gave that speech that left me floored.
Lewis MacAdams and John Godfrey wandered in from Buffalo
In search of the Boston Sound, which didn't actually exist,
Though we discovered "Sister Ray" instead. Winter into spring
And days of wondering what to do about the draft.
John arrived again, and we spent most of spring vacation
Stoned, and wrote a hundred poems—the less said of which
The better—and finally June arrived, and I went back to California
To get married, and in September moved to Porter Square.

All this came rushing back to me at once, and at first
I had no idea why. Then suddenly I remembered
That the spring before I moved to Cambridge
I'd competed in a poetry contest at Mt. Holyoke
(John drove me, come to think of it), that in a small way

Saved my life, though that's a story for another day.

There were three distinguished judges, avatars

Of what you wanted to become when you grew up

If genius smiled on you, or you were lucky and persistent.

Last week I got a letter asking me to be a judge

In next year's contest, and I realized the guy who wrote it

Was the same poor soul who'd had to suffer through that evening

At the *Advocate* almost exactly forty years ago.

In my beginning is my end. We poets in our youth . . .

I had a hollow feeling of completion, as though a circle had closed

And I'd become what I'd aspired to—without despondency or
    madness

To be sure, but without any real satisfaction either, and certainly

Without ever growing up. Do people ever really *change*?

John's a nurse in New York, Lewis lives in California, David in Florida,

All at it in their own ways I suppose. I've no idea where Ed is,

Though I'm sure he's persevering too. Lucky or unlucky,

Bedecked with laurels or languishing in obscurity,

The fact is that we're older, just as time, for all its deceptive

Symmetries, moves in one direction towards one end.

You try to cheat it, finding signs of life, of promises fulfilled,

In what are merely randomness and age, withdrawing from the world

Into a naive dream of art, or of a shared imagination,

But it's never convincing. Sitting on a bar stool in an airport,

Waiting for a flight to take me to a reading, I sometimes

Think that Dan was right in what he meant—that what passes

For ambition and accomplishment is mostly vanity, vanity

And self-indulgence, if not quite in the sense he'd had in mind.

It's all, as Yeats remarked, a silent quarrel with yourself,
One in which internal strife and external equanimity
Cancel each other out, presenting to the world
About the last thing it needs—another modern poet,
One more poor bastard at the wrong end of life.

THIS IS LAGOS

. . . hope would be hope for the wrong thing

—T. S. Eliot

Instead of the usual welcoming sign to greet you
There's the brute statement: *This is Lagos.*
If you make it to the island—if you make your way
Across the bridge and past the floating slums
And sawmills and the steaming garbage dumps, the auto yards
Still burning with spilled fuel and to your final destination
At the end of a long tracking shot, all of it on fire—
You come face-to-face with hell: the pandemonium
Of history's ultimate bazaar, a breathing mass
Whose cells are stalls crammed full of spare parts,
Chains, detergents, DVDs; where a continuous cacophony
Of yells and radios and motorcycles clogs the air.
They arrive from everywhere, attracted by the promise
Of mere possibility, by the longing for a different kind of day

Here in the city of scams, by a hope that quickly comes to nothing.
To some it's a new paradigm, "an announcement of the future"
Where disorder leads to unexpected patterns, unimagined
     opportunities
That mutate, blossom, and evolve. To others it's the face of despair.
These are the parameters of life, a life doled out in quarters,
In the new, postmodern state of nature: garbage and ground plastic
And no place to shit or sleep; machetes, guns, and e-mails
Sent around the world from Internet cafés; violence and chaos
And a self-effacing sprawl that simply makes no sense
When seen from ground zero, yet exhibits an abstract beauty
When seen from the air—which is to say, not seen at all.

Across the ocean and a century away a culture died.
The facts behind the Crow's whole way of life—the sense
Of who and what they were, their forms of excellence and bravery
And honor—all dissolved, and their hearts "fell to the ground,
And they could not lift them up again. After this nothing happened"
(Plenty Coups), meaning nothing they could do made any sense,
Beyond the fact of biological survival. It's easy to forget
How much of ordinary life, of what we value, long for, and recall—
Ambition, admiration, even poetry—rests on things we take for granted,
And how fragile those things are. "I am trying to live a life I do not
     understand,"
A woman said, when the buffalo and the coups they underwrote
     were gone.
They could have tried to cope. Instead they found their solace
In an indeterminate hope, a hope for a future they couldn't yet
     imagine,

Where their ways of life might somehow reemerge in forms
Of which they couldn't yet conceive, or even begin to understand.
It was a dream of a different life, a life beyond the reservation
Without any tangible location, predicated on a new idea of the good
With no idea of what it was, or what achieving it might mean—
Like listening to a song with no sound, or drawing an imaginary line
In the imaginary sand in an imaginary world without boundaries.

It feels compelling, and I even think it's true. But these are things
I've only read about in magazines and book reviews, and not
    experienced,
Which was Plato's point—that poets don't know what they talk about.
It doesn't matter though, for most of what we think of as our lives
Is lived in the imagination, like the Crow's inchoate hope, or the
    fantasies
Of those who leave a village in the country for the city in the smoke.
And when I look in *my* imagination for the future, it isn't hope and
    restoration
That I find but smoldering tires and con men in a world of megacities
And oil fields, where too much has been annexed to be restored.
I have the luxury of an individual life that has its own trajectory
    and scope
When taken on its terms—the terms I chose—however
    unimportant it might seem
From the vantage point of history or the future. What scares me is
    the thought
That in a world that isn't far away this quaint ideal of the personal
Is going to disappear, dissolving in those vast, impersonal calculations

Through which money, the ultimate abstraction, renders each life
    meaningless,
By rendering the forms of life that make it seem significant impossible.
Face me I face you: packed into rooms with concrete beds
And not a trace of privacy, subsisting on contaminated water, luck,
And palm-wine gin, with lungs scarred from the burning air,
These are the urban destitute, the victims of a gospel of prosperity
Untouched by irony or nostalgia—for how can you discover
What you haven't felt, or feel the loss of things you've never known?
I write because I can: talking to myself, composing poems
And wondering what you'll make of them; shoring them
Against the day our minor ways of life have finally disappeared
And we're not even ghosts. Meanwhile life regresses
Towards the future, death by death. You to whom I write,
Or wish that I could write long after my own death,
When it's too late to talk to you about the world you live in,
This is the world you live in: This is Lagos.

NINETY-FIFTH STREET

Words can bang around in your head
Forever, if you let them and you give them room.
I used to love poetry, and mostly I still do,
Though sometimes "I, too, dislike it." There must be
Something real beyond the fiddle and perfunctory
Consolations and the quarrels—as of course
There is, though what it is is difficult to say.
The salt is on the briar rose, the fog is in the fir trees.
I didn't know what it was, and I don't know now,
But it was what I started out to do, and now, a lifetime later,
All I've really done. *The Opening of the Field,*
Roots and Branches, Rivers and Mountains: I sat in my room
Alone, their fragments shored against the ruin or revelation
That was sure to come, breathing in their secret atmosphere,
Repeating them until they almost seemed my own.
We like to think our lives are what they study to become,
And yet so much of life is waiting, waiting on a whim.
So much of what we are is sheer coincidence,
Like a sentence whose significance is retrospective,

Made up out of elementary particles that are in some sense
Simply sounds, like syllables that finally settle into place.
You probably think that this is a poem about poetry
(And obviously it is), yet its real subject is time,
For that's what poetry is—a way to live through time
And sometimes, just for a while, to bring it back.

➜ ❧

A paneled dining room in Holder Hall. Stage right, enter twit:
"Mr. Ashbery, I'm your biggest campus fan." We hit it off
And talked about "The Skaters" and my preference for "Clepsydra"
Vs. "Fragment." Later on that night John asked me to a party in
   New York,
And Saturday, after dinner and a panel on the artist's role as something
(And a party), driving Lewis's Austin-Healey through the rain
I sealed our friendship with an accident. The party was on Broadway,
An apartment (white of course, with paintings) just downstairs
From Frank O'Hara's, who finally wandered down. I talked to him
A little about *Love Poems (Tentative Title)*, which pleased him,
And quoted a line from "Poem" about the rain, which seemed to
   please him too.
The party ended, John and I went off to Max's, ordered steaks,
And talked about our mothers. All that talking!—poems and
   paintings,
Parents, all those parties, and the age of manifestos still to come!
I started coming to New York for lunch. We'd meet at *Art News*,
Walk to Fifty-sixth Street to Larré's, a restaurant filled with French
   expatriates,
Have martinis and the prix fixe for $2.50 (!), drink rosé de Provence,

And talk (of course) about Genet and James and words like
   "Coca-Cola."
It was an afternoon in May when John brought up a play
That he and Kenneth Koch and Frank O'Hara—Holy Trinity!
(*Batman* was in vogue)—had started years ago and never finished.
There was a dictator named Edgar and some penicillin,
But that's all I remember. They hadn't actually been together
In years, but planned to finish it that night at John's new apartment
On Ninety-fifth Street, and he said to come by for a drink
Before they ate and got to work. It was a New York dream
Come true: a brownstone floor-through, white and full of paintings
(Naturally), "with a good library and record collection."
John had procured a huge steak, and as I helped him set the table
The doorbell rang and Frank O'Hara, fresh from the museum
And svelte in a houndstooth sports coat entered, followed shortly
By "excitement-prone Kenneth Koch" in somber gray,
And I was one with my immortals. In the small mythologies
We make up out of memories and the flow of time
A few moments remain frozen, though the feel of them is lost,
The feel of talk. It ranged from puns to gossip, always coming back
To poems and poets. Frank was fiercely loyal to young poets
(Joe Ceravolo's name came up I think), and when I mentioned Lewis
In a way that must have sounded catty, he leaped to his defense,
Leaving me to backtrack in embarrassment and have another drink,
Which is what everyone had. I think you see where it was going:
Conversation drifting into dinner, then I stayed for dinner
And everyone forgot about the play, which was never finished
(Though I think I've seen a fragment of it somewhere). I see a table
In a cone of light, but there's no sound except for Kenneth's

Deadpan "Love to see a boy eat" as I speared a piece of steak;
And then the only voice I'm sure I hear is mine,
As those moments that had once seemed singular and clear
Dissolve into a "general mess of imprecision of feeling"
And images, augmented by line breaks. There were phone calls,
Other people arrived, the narrative of the night dissolved,
And finally everyone went home. School and spring wound down.
The semester ended, then the weekend that I wrote about in
   "Sally's Hair"
Arrived and went, and then a late-night cruise around Manhattan
   for a rich friend's
Parents' anniversary bash, followed by an Upper East Side preppie bar
That left me looking for a place to crash, and so I rang John's bell
   at 2 a.m.
And failed (thank God) to rouse him, caught a plane to San Diego
The next day, worked at my summer job and worked on poems
And started reading Proust, and got a card one afternoon
From Peter Schjeldahl telling me that Frank O'Hara had been killed.

Ninety-fifth Street soldiered on for several years.
I remember a cocktail party (the symposium of those days),
Followed by dinner just around the corner at Elaine's,
Pre–Woody Allen. It was there I learned of RFK's assassination
When I woke up on the daybed in the living room, and where
John told me getting married would ruin me as a poet
(I don't know why—most of his friends were married), a judgment
He revised when he met Susan and inscribed *The Double Dream
   of Spring*
"If this is all we need fear from spinach, then I don't mind so much"

(Which was probably premature—watering his plants one day
She soaked his landlord, Giorgio Cavallon, dozing in the garden below).
It was where Peter Delacorte late one night recited an entire side
Of a Firesign Theatre album from memory, and set John on *that*
    path,
To his friends' subsequent dismay, and where he blessed me with
    his extra copy
Of *The Poems*, and next day had second thoughts (though I kept it
    anyway).
Sometimes a vague, amorphous stretch of years assumes a shape,
And then becomes an age, and then a golden age alive with possibilities,
When change was in the air and you could wander through its streets
As though through Florence and the Renaissance. I know it sounds
    ridiculous,
But that's the way life flows: in stages that take form in retrospect,
When all the momentary things that occupy the mind from day to day
Have vanished into time, and something takes their place that
    wasn't there,
A sense of freedom—one that gradually slipped away. The center
Of the conversation moved downtown, the Renaissance gave way to
    mannerism
As the junior faculty took charge, leaving the emeriti alone and out
    of it
Of course, lying on the fringes, happily awake; but for the rest
The laws proscribing what you couldn't do were clear. I got so tired
Of writing all those New York poems (though by then I'd moved to
    Boston—
To Siena, you might say) that led to nowhere but the next one,
So I started writing poems about whatever moved me: what it's *like*

To be alive within a world that holds no place for you, yet seems so
    beautiful;
The feeling of the future, and its disappointments; the trajectory of
    a life,
That always brought me back to time and memory (I'd finished
    Proust by then),
And brings me back to this. John finally moved downtown himself,
Into a two-story apartment at Twenty-fifth and Tenth, with a spiral
    staircase
Leading to a library, the locus of the incident of Susan, Alydar, and
    John
And the pitcher of water (I'll draw a veil over it), and Jimmy
    Schuyler sighing
"It's so *beautiful*," as Bernadette Peters sang "Raining in My Heart"
    from *Dames at Sea*.
The poetry still continued—mine and everyone's. I'd added Jimmy
To my pantheon (as you've probably noticed), but the night in
    nineteen sixty-six
Seemed more and more remote: I never saw Kenneth anymore,
And there were new epicenters, with new casts of characters, like
    Madoo,
Bob Dash's garden in Sagaponack, and Bill and Willy's loft in Soho.
John moved again, to Twenty-second Street, and Susan and I moved
    to Milwaukee,
Where our son was born. I stopped coming to New York, and
    writing poems,
For several years, while I tried to dream enough philosophy for
    tenure.
One afternoon in May I found myself at Ninth and Twenty-second,

And as though on cue two people whom I hadn't seen in years—
    David Kalstone,
Darragh Park—just happened by, and then I took a taxi down to
    SoHo
To the loft, and then a gallery to hear Joe Brainard read from "I
    Remember,"
Back to John's and out to dinner—as though I'd never been away,
Though it was all too clear I had. Poems were in the air, but theory
    too,
And members of the thought police department (who must have
    also gotten tenure)
Turned up everywhere, with arguments that poetry was called upon
    to prove.
It mattered, but in a different way, as though it floated free from
    poems
And wasn't quite the point. I kept on coming back, as I still do.
Half my life was still to come, and yet the rest was mostly personal:
I got divorced, and Willy killed himself, and here I am now, ready
    to retire.
There was an obituary in the *Times* last week for Michael Goldberg,
A painter you'll recall from Frank O'Hara's poems ("Why I Am
    Not a Painter,"
"Ode to Michael Goldberg's (Birth and Other Births)"). I didn't
    know him,
But a few months after the soiree on Ninety-fifth Street I was at a party
In his studio on the Bowery, which was still his studio when he died.
The New York art world demimonde was there, including nearly
    everyone

Who's turned up in this poem. I remember staring at a guy who
Looked like something from the Black Lagoon, dancing with a
    gorgeous
Woman half his age. That's *my* New York: an island dream
Of personalities and evenings, nights where poetry was second nature
And their lives flowed through it and around it as it gave them life.
O brave new world (now old) that had such people in't!

⇥ ⇤

"The tiresome old man is telling us his life story."
I guess I am, but that's what poets do—not always
Quite as obviously as this, and usually more by indirection
And omission, but beneath the poetry lies the singular reality
And unreality of an individual life. I see it as a long
Illuminated tunnel, lined with windows giving on the scenes
    outside—
A city and a countryside, some dormitory rooms, that night
On Ninety-fifth Street forty years ago. As life goes on
You start to get increasingly distracted by your own reflection
And the darkness gradually becoming visible at the end.
I try not to look too far ahead, but just to stay here—
Quick now, here, now, always—only something pulls me
Back (as they say) to the day, when poems were more like secrets,
With their own vernacular, and you could tell your friends
By who and what they read. And now John's practically become
A national treasure, and whenever I look up I think I see him
Floating in the sky like the Cheshire Cat. I don't know
What to make of it, but it makes me happy—like seeing Kenneth
Just before he died ("I'm going west John, I'm going west")

In his apartment on a side street near Columbia, or remembering
Once again that warm spring night in nineteen sixty-six.
I like to think of them together once again, at the cocktail party
At the end of the mind, where I could blunder in and ruin it one
    last time.
Meanwhile, on a hillside in the driftless region to the west,
A few miles from the small town where *The Straight Story* ends,
I'm building a house on a meadow, if I'm permitted to return,
Behind a screen of trees above a lower meadow, with some apple
    trees
In which the fog collects on autumn afternoons, and a vista
Of an upland pasture without heaviness. I see myself
Sitting on the deck and sipping a martini, as I used to at Larré's,
In a future that feels almost like a past I'm positive is there—
But where? I think my life is still all conversation,
Only now it's with myself. I can see it continuing forever,
Even in my absence, as I close the windows and turn off the lights
And it begins to rain. And then we're there together
In the house on the meadow, waiting for whatever's left to come
In what's become the near future—two versions of myself
And of the people that we knew, each one an other
To the other, yet both indelibly there: the twit of twenty
And the aging child of sixty-two, still separate
And searching in the night, listening through the night
To the noise of the rain and memories of rain
And evenings when we'd wander out into the Renaissance,
When I could see you and talk to you and it could still *change*;
And still there in the morning when the rain has stopped,
And the apples are all getting tinted in the cool light.

BOOKS BY JOHN KOETHE

FALLING WATER
Poems

ISBN 0-06-095257-1 (paperback)

"As funny and fresh as it is tragic and undeceived, *Falling Water* ranks with Wallace Stevens' *Auroras of Autumn* as one of the profoundest meditations on existence ever formulated by an American poet." —John Ashbery

THE CONSTRUCTOR
Poems

ISBN 0-06-095635-6 (paperback)

"*The Constructor* is a scrupulous, elegant account of the meditative intellect as an instrument continually registering the passage of time. Exquisitely modulated and brutally honest, these poems would be harrowing were they not so seductively beautiful." —George Bradley

NORTH POINT NORTH
New and Selected Poems

ISBN 0-06-093527-8 (paperback)

"John Koethe's meditative poems have a tranquility which is both enchanting and deceptive: once inside the maze of his mind, we enter more and more worlds. Or is it the other way around? Mind into the world mind: dreamy, absorbing, alarming, these are poems to lose and find oneself in." —Rachel Hadas

SALLY'S HAIR
Poems

ISBN 0-06-117627-3 (paperback)

"A highly readable book, appealing in its elusive and somewhat eerie blend of the personal and impersonal, and compelling in the rigor of its inquiry into the human condition." —*Boston Review*

"Passionate, lyrical poems of great energy and provocative ideas."
—*Entertainment Weekly*